The Best and Worst 50 Sexual Experiences Ever

The Best and Worst 50 Sexual Experiences Ever

K. Marie
Copyright © 2015 K. Marie Publishing

Thank you for respecting the work of this author. No part of this book may be reproduced or transmitted by any means without the written permission of the author. The unauthorized distribution or reproduction of this copyrighted work is illegal. All rights reserved.

ISBN-13: 978-0692382929

The Best and Worst 50 Sexual Experiences Ever

DEDICATION

This book is dedicated to all of the single and married people that love to have great sex without the headache of feeling trapped after it's all over.

The
Best and Worst
50
Sexual Experiences
Ever

THE BEST AND WORST 50 SEXUAL EXPERIENCES EVER

The Best and Worst 50 Sexual Experiences Ever

CONTENTS

Chapter 1: The Best Sexual Experiences

Chapter 2: The Worst Sexual Experiences

Chapter 3: Personal Sex Journal

Chapter 4: Monthly Sex Goals To Spice Up My Sex Life

The Best and Worst 50 Sexual Experiences Ever

ACKNOWLEDGEMENTS

God for blessing me, my lovely daughters, my parents, my sister and brother, my grandparents and my cousin Troy last but not least Me, Myself and I and every negative person I have met in my life including some negative family members. You make me want to work harder and never give up daily. I want to say thanks to Charmaine and Sheena Bryant and Laroya Morris, Nikki Harris and the Basement in Atlanta and S.Marriam you are truly my family and I'm grateful we have all been apart of each others life for more than 10 years. Last but not least Mr.Judah thanks for always being a true friend. Every day is a new beginning and anything is possible. Regardless of the negativity that may be around you. Kandi said "fly above the haters". Just keep moving forward.

THE
BEST AND WORST
50
SEXUAL EXPERIENCES
EVER

The Best and Worst 50 Sexual Experiences Ever

CHAPTER 1
THE
BEST
SEXUAL EXPERIENCES

The Best and Worst 50 Sexual Experiences Ever

Best Lovers

1.Sexual Fluent Language Speaker

Description: While having hot passionate intense love making, your partner suddenly start to speak another language during sex than their original language rather it's Spanish, Chinese, tongue or just start cursing.

Have you ever had a Sexual Fluent language speaker? What language did they speak originally and because the sex was so good what language did they start speaking?

_____
_____
_____
_____

The Best and Worst 50 Sexual Experiences Ever

2. Aggressive Love Maker

Description: A person that love to have aggressive sex. You love to have your hair pulled or you love to get spanked while getting fucked hard. You like to be whipped and slightly choked or bitten. You have no shame in being the giver or the receiver.

Are you an Aggressive Love Maker? Or would you rather be the one being taken control of?

_____
_____
_____
_____

The Best and Worst 50 Sexual Experiences Ever

3. Undercover Lover

Description: Classy and quiet teacher, business owner, and doctor or dentist maybe even your local politician and pastors by day and a nasty porno freak at night. Basically this lover is self explanatory. They are in uniform and suits during the day and at night they are your dominatrix sex slave that loves hand cuffs, whips and chains. They love all types of freaky nasty things. The freak comes out of them in the evening, trade the politician suit and tie in for a trapeze swinger club membership.

Have you had a sexual encounter with an undercover lover? What was their daytime career? What was the open minded freak they turned into after the day of work was over? Describe even if you are the undercover lover.

_____
_____
_____

The Best and Worst 50 Sexual Experiences Ever

4. Hopeless Romantic

Description: A wonderful romantic man or women that love to bring home flowers, run your bath water, massage your body with your favorite oil from head to toe. All after a hard day at work without you even have to ask them to these wonderful things for you. They hold you until you fall asleep, with or without the sex. Make you breakfast in bed in the morning. They write you sexy and thoughtful love letters. Take you on romantic getaways just because they care. He or she is that person who has something special for you on any given day, just to show you how much they truly care and to show how much they appreciate you for being in their life.

What are some of the most romantic things someone ever did for you? Did you appreciate them or did you take them for granted?

_____
_____
_____
_____

The Best and Worst 50 Sexual Experiences Ever

5. Thug Lover

Description: A person that may have a lot of sexy tattoos or piercings. A person that may talk a little slang, they may be the one to press your back down while fucking you from the back so your ass won't move. He or she wants to keep that nice arch in your back. He or she put you straight to sleep with a long hard dick and body exhausting moves. Basically, it's someone that can take control and fuck the hell out of you. He may smoke a joint while he fucks you, he may offer to pass it back and forth while you're fucking each other or ask you to sip champagne or sip Avion tequila with him while you're riding his dick and lick it off your hard nipples.

Where was your Thug Lover from? What outrageous techniques or moves have they used to put you straight to sleep?

_____
_____
_____
_____

The Best and Worst 50 Sexual Experiences Ever

6. Sexual Expert

Description: A person who thinks they know everything about having sex, they know all of the sex positions all of the new and old toys to make you cum. They may have even watch the Dr. Sue Sex Show and a lot of porn just to keep up with the latest sex moves and the details on how to pleasure your partner. They know where your g spot is and how to make you squirt and still leave you wanting more.

Who is the Sexual Expert in your life? What sex toys or sex positions do you want to explore while with your Sex Expert?

_____
_____
_____

The Best and Worst 50 Sexual Experiences Ever

7. Sex Fein

Description: A male or female that loves to have sex constantly at least four or five time a day. Their day will not be complete unless they engage in some type of sexual activity with themselves, a spouse or even at random times.

Please don't confuse this description with being a sex addict someone with a bad addiction that need to seek medical help or therapy. Do you have a sex fene you love to have sex with? How many times do they like to fuck daily?

_____
_____
_____

The Best and Worst 50 Sexual Experiences Ever

8. Spontaneous Lover

Description: Love to have sex anytime or any place. They may want to have sex at the movies, restaurant, park or even on the side of the road in the car. My favorite is a golf course or receiving oral sex while driving. You never know what to expect from a spontaneous lover. My ultimate sex spot would be to get fucked while in a hot air balloon while looking at the beautiful scenery, or to get fucked while going up and down on a roller coaster. I haven't figured out when this could happen yet but hopefully one day soon. Don't be afraid to try something new. You may actually like it.

Who is your Spontaneous lover? What are the most Spontaneous places you ever had sex at? Where are your dream fucking or love making spots?

_____
_____
_____
_____

The Best and Worst 50 Sexual Experiences Ever

9. Make up Sex

Description: When you have an awful disagreement or argument with your lover, spouse, fuck partner and you have a conversation and make up while having sex, fucking or love making. Yes people it is a difference in the three types. When the sex is over everything may be all better or just better for the moment. This can be a great start to healing and fixing whatever the issue was that caused the fight. So get to fucking so you can cry and take out your anger and frustrations on the dick or while you're in the pussy.

_____
_____
_____
_____

The Best and Worst 50 Sexual Experiences Ever

10.Drunk Sex

Description: When you clearly have had more drinks than you can handle and you are at a club, home or a your favorite restaurant. You start to feel instantly emotional and start thinking of that special someone you miss emotionally or sexually and you have suddenly built up the courage to text or call them after you have gotten drunk. You let all your emotions known and you don't care because you're drunk. Sometimes this may end up being a disaster and other times this will end up with an invite or a visit from the lover you just had the courage to call. You then will see them and have passionate unforgettable sex courtesy of your favorite choice of liquor you was drinking.

Have you had passionate drunk sex? How was it? Do you regret having it or was it one of the best nights you ever had sexually?

_____
_____
_____
_____

The Best and Worst 50 Sexual Experiences Ever

11. Cum Expert

Description: A cum expert makes you cum like no other has ever made you have an orgasm before. A cum expert makes your leg shake beyond your control. While you're receiving oral sex, during sex and while you have an orgasm. A cum expert know how to hit all your favorite spots and they know exactly what to do to make your toes curl. Rather it's from oral sex or intercourse.

What are your hot spots? What parts on your body your mate can touch that makes your toes curl?

_____
_____
_____

The Best and Worst 50 Sexual Experiences Ever

12. Fantasy Lover

Description: Fantasy lover is someone you finally had sex with after wishing and fantasizing about them. Your fantasy lover maybe someone at your job, your church or even in your local Starbucks that work at the counter. Even a celebrity that you thought you would never meet and somehow you finally crossed paths. When you woke up the next morning and you saw them lying next to you, you thought you were dreaming. But it wasn't. Basically it was a dream that came true.

What celebrity or person would be your ideal Fantasy Lover? If you could have one night only who would you choose to be your fantasy lover for the evening?

_____
_____
_____

The Best and Worst 50 Sexual Experiences Ever

13. Chin Hair Lover

Description: Guys with a chin hair or a beard when he kisses you. The hair on his chin tickles your chin. When he gives you oral sex you're wet juices get all over his mouth and into his beard or chin hair. When he comes up for air and he kisses you your mouth is wet also. Personally love it, it turns me on.

Do you rather have a clean cut or a chin hair lover? Do you mind the juices on his beard when he comes up for air during oral sex?

_____
_____
_____
_____

The Best and Worst 50 Sexual Experiences Ever

14. Breakup Sex

Description: All of us have had this before. This is the last time you and you're partner will make love. So you fuck the shit out of each other like never before and you release all of the emotions that you have built up for that person from the past, present and future thoughts of being without them. You both give it all you got because you know this will be the last time you will feel each other. Every experience you have had with this person will flash before your eyes in your mind while you're making love. You may even shed a tear or two.

When you had breakup sex, was it just that or did you ever go back?

_____
_____
_____

The Best and Worst 50 Sexual Experiences Ever

15. Best Kisser

Description: This person has the perfect shaped sexy beautiful lips you have ever seen and kissed. They stay licking them because they know the sexual damage they can do with those sexy ass lips. Their lips are never ashy or chapped. Every time you kiss them it feel perfect, it's like you are in a movie. Just looking at them makes you horny and ready for some action. They know exactly how to use the sexy lips and also the kisses are just right.

Who is your best kisser?

_____
_____
_____
_____

The Best and Worst 50 Sexual Experiences Ever

16. Hate You Sex

Description: Someone you may be in a relationship with or someone you don't even like or you cannot stand to really be around. You constantly argue with this person and you fight twenty two hours out of the day. The other two hours you are fucking them because you have nothing else in common with them. Unfortunately that is the only time that you can connect with them.

If you ever been in this situation before, how was the situation handled? After the sex was over was it an awkward feeling?

_____
_____
_____
_____

The Best and Worst 50 Sexual Experiences Ever

17. Fun Sex

Description: You love having sex with this person it is never a dull moment when they enter in the bedroom. They always have the best fun items in the bedroom. Your spouse may have fun vibrators such as the rabbit, bullet and remote control panties. Sexy one of a kind glass toys from K. Marie Intimates. Various props such as handcuffs, blindfolds, candle wax, a sex swing, whip cream and chocolate, even pasties from the K. Marie Intimates collection. They always aim to please.

What are some of your favorite items used in the bedroom? What Item or items you would like to use in the bedroom?

_____
_____
_____
_____

The Best and Worst 50 Sexual Experiences Ever

18. Affectionate Lover

Description: You have a partner that gaze into your eyes while you're making love. Kiss every part of your body and hold you close. An affectionate lover care about your feelings, they are concerned with your wants and needs inside and outside of the bedroom. The job for an affectionate lover is not complete until they satisfy you and make you cum. They also get up and run your shower or get the wet warm towel to clean you up after the love making is complete. They also snuggle with you afterwards.

What was the nicest way your affectionate lover expressed their emotions for you during or after sex?

_____
_____
_____
_____

The Best and Worst 50 Sexual Experiences Ever

19. Out Of Town Lover

Description: Out of town lover stay a couple of hours away or in a another state. They have no problem with traveling to come and see you in the time of sexual or emotional need. Every time you meet your out of town lover you know they are coming with a special delivery. When they call you and arrive you suddenly smile because you automatically know what time it is. When you're out of town lover come to visit it's really no time to debate or argue. Every moment will be special because the time you have to spend with each other is limited.

What cities do you think have some of the sexiest men and women?

_____
_____
_____
_____

The Best and Worst 50 Sexual Experiences Ever

20. Imaginary Lover

Description: Imaginary lover is someone you wish you can make love to, but you cannot. More than likely you don't know them or you see them often but they are already married or in a relationship so basically off limits. So you go home and fantasize and masturbate while thinking about them. You may even go all out and give your sex toy a nick name. The same name of that special sexy someone you fantasize about. You may even use your imagination to and pretend in your mind they are that sexy person you fantasize daily about while you are making love to your current mate. You fuck your partner and pretend they are the person you want but you cannot have.

Have you ever done this before? Have you ever had an unattainable? How about an Imaginary Lover? Have you ever wished your spouse was someone other than themselves while you were making love to them?

_____
_____
_____

The Best and Worst 50 Sexual Experiences Ever

21. Well Endowed Big Dick Lover

Definition: A lover with a huge penis. Most women and some men want a well endowed lover. At least that is what they say. But what happens when he is too well endowed and you get nervous at the sight of his penis. It can be very overwhelming. Just to know that you have to deep throat that big dick and ride it and take it like a solider while he fucking you from the back. Personally, I love it. I love a exciting challenge of course a couple shots of tequila courage juice can help a lot. Then before you know it you will be taking the dick like a pro.

Do you prefer a well endowed lover a medium or a small penis lover? Why?

_____
_____
_____
_____

The Best and Worst 50 Sexual Experiences Ever

22. Energizer Bunny Lover

Definition: He or She loves to have sex for hours without any type of break. Sometimes your partner may even ask you to cum because they are exhausted and need a break or they may fake a bathroom break just to give themselves a minor rest without disappointing you.

Has this ever happen to you before? Have you had a lover that wanted to keep going and going and going?

_____
_____
_____
_____

The Best and Worst 50 Sexual Experiences Ever

23. Uncircumcised Penis

Definition: A sexy man that has a penis with fore skin protecting his penis. This is a very controversial topic. Many men and women like a Circumcised penis others do not. Myself personally I love all types of penis. Rather it's circumcised or not, as long as it can get a erection that's the most important thing. So what if you have to pull a little skin back to get to the ultimate surprise inside, I don't know about you but I love sexy surprises.

What is your preference? Do you rather have sex with a man with a circumcised or uncircumcised penis? Why this preference?
_____
_____
_____
_____

The Best and Worst 50 Sexual Experiences Ever

Who are your best sexual lovers on the best list? What lover or lovers on the list can you relate to and why?

_____
_____
_____
_____
_____
_____
_____
_____

THE BEST AND WORST 50 SEXUAL EXPERIENCES EVER

The Best and Worst 50 Sexual Experiences Ever

CHAPTER 2
THE
WORST
SEXUAL EXPERIENCES

The Best and Worst 50 Sexual Experiences Ever

25. LEFT OVER LOVER

Description: A left over lover is basically what it sounds like. A left over lover is someone else's leftovers. Basically, someone you know that use to date your best friend, a close family member, a teammate, band member and now that they are broken up you could not wait to date them or fuck them or even possibly marry them. Now you are sleeping with your family member ex lover, both of you dipping in the same pot or licking the same lollipop. Some of you settle for leftovers because you feel like you don't want or you may feel you can't get anyone better. Truly there are so many men and women in the world to settle for someone else leftovers. Yes, I'm saying there are millions of people in the world a portion is married, half of the people of damage goods and not even worth saying hello to or not even worth looking at. The rest are single and that will end in heartbreak and disappointment and the possible 2% left is actually a great catch and your life partner. Yes ladies and gentleman it's fucked up out here. Dating sucks but unfortunately we have to do it to meet that special person we want to share our life with.

The Best and Worst 50 Sexual Experiences Ever

Have you ever dated a family member or close friend ex before? How about a teammate or co-worker ex even though you felt that shit was so damn wrong? Was the outcome worth it? Was the sex at least what you thought it would be? If your family member, close friend or co-worker found out, what was their reaction?

_____
_____
_____
_____

The Best and Worst 50 Sexual Experiences Ever

26. Psycho Lover

Description: When you're dating a person that is just plain crazy. Going on dates with them is amazing you always have a great time when you are out, you have reached that fourth date and the chemistry is impeccable. This person understands you and you fully understand them. But as soon as you make the decision to have sex with them from that point on from the morning after they turn into a psychotic individual you don't even know. You dated for about a couple of weeks or so. You have sex with them and they start saying baby I love you. You're looking like damn it's only been a short while we had been dating and we only have slept together once. They become an instant overnight psycho. They start to constantly call or text you. Even if you don't answer they call just to listen to your voice on your voice mail recording. They become very, very clingy. They will pop up at your house or job possibly even your family or friends house after you do not answer your phone. They will drive by your house to see if your truly home like you claim to be. They will even sit and wait outside your home to watch who is going in and out your house to make sure your not cheating on

The Best and Worst 50 Sexual Experiences Ever

them. Psycho lover full time job becomes keeping track on you. The sad part is that they don't realize that they have turned instantly crazy overnight and that they have lost their damn mind.

Have you ever been or had a psycho lover before? What are some things that was said or done that was crazy? If you had a psycho lover what was something that was done to get away and break up with them?

_____
_____
_____
_____

The Best and Worst 50 Sexual Experiences Ever

27. Insecure Lover

Description: Insecure lover is a lover that is insecure with themselves or their sexuality. They don't like to have sex with the light on. The insecure lover hate to have their lover see them naked. They have sex with clothes on to hide a certain parts of their body they are not happy with rather is a shirt a bra, socks anything that can help hide their insecurities. You may think they are the sexiest person alive but their personal insecurities in the bedroom and outside the bedroom take a toll on the relationship which eventually is the cause of the break up. Outside the bedroom when you are on a date or out in public they may think you are looking at another man or women and your being very disrespectful when in actuality you are not even looking at anyone. Or every time your phone ring and they here the opposite sex on the other end they get an attitude because they think you're cheating.

What are some actions your insecure lover has shown you to prove that they are insecure with themselves or the relationship? Are you insecure about any physical part of your body and has it

The Best and Worst 50 Sexual Experiences Ever

interfered with your sex life?

_____
_____
_____
_____

The Best and Worst 50 Sexual Experiences Ever

29. All bad (Just Negative Lover)

Description: This person emotionally stresses you out constantly. They are never there for you. They never lend any emotional support when needed. They actually treat you bad emotionally they may even verbally abuse you and make you feel like you're a loser or a horrible person. They constantly sleep with others and cheat on you. They may even be honest and admit they are cheating on you. A all bad lover do not take you on any dates nor give you any quality time. Rather it's because they claim they are busy or they just clearly tell you that they don't want to take you on dates. Unfortunately even after all of these things you still want to fuck them and be with them. You constantly choose to make excuses for them even though you know you deserve better. You are living in complete denial and waiting and hoping things will change. Before you know it years had passed and they are the same person you are still lonely and unhappy and your vagina or penis and even mouth is all worn out from the constant sex that you have given a undeserving human being. Now you are all bitter and used up because you have given your complete all to a Ass hole that didn't appreciate the cooking,

The Best and Worst 50 Sexual Experiences Ever

cleaning, doing their dirty ass laundry and all the time you spend fucking them and giving them head like a good mate should. Unfortunately when that special right one come around you feel guarded and you have walls up giving them a hard time. Because you feel unworthy of being loved because you gave so much away in your previous relationship and you hurt so much you can't realize when that special someone come along and they just want to love you and make you happy. Eventually you will break and give in or you will lose them because of your anger and bitterness from your past fucked up relationship with the all bad lover.

Are you in a relationship with a all bad lover now? If so wake up and get rid of them. Move on with your life that relationship or situation is a DEAD END.

_____
_____
_____
_____

The Best and Worst 50 Sexual Experiences Ever

30. GOOD ON PAPER (BUT BAD IN BED)

Description: A man or women that has amazing credit or someone that is financially stable hard working. They have completed college and they may have a masters or a doctorate degree to be, they have completed countless amounts of community service and they have earn many accolades to show for all the hard work and effort in the corporate or business world. So from the outside looking in you're amazed at their accomplishments and success. You start to date this individual and eventually you finally have sex with them. After all the admiring the time to express your sexual emotions is here. Sex is over and you feel like you just wasted your time, your gas and a great pair of panties or underwear for a sorry not even mediocre sexual disaster. You can't even say it was an experience. The sex was terrible! The sex was so terrible you didn't even stay the night you just put your clothes on and left.
If you have a bit of heart or emotion left for them you may have even made a crazy excuse to why you have to leave right after having sex with them just not to hurt their feelings. Regardless what the objective is to get out of there immediately and

The Best and Worst 50 Sexual Experiences Ever

never come back. Fortunately for you, you have a chance to save your sex life so it wouldn't crash and burn with the person you just had the worst sex with. So you never contacted them again.
Have you ever had a person that had a great personality and an amazing and great career and the sex was WACK? What did you do? Stay and work out the bad sex or give up and bailed out of the relationship or stayed in the relationship and just had sex with someone you were sexual compatible with?

_____
_____
_____
_____

The Best and Worst 50 Sexual Experiences Ever

32. SWEATY LOVER

Description: This lover sweats on you like crazy during sex. I'm not talking about a couple of drops after about 30 minutes of fucking. I'm talking about 10 minutes of pounding or dick riding and instantly as you lay there it feels like someone just dumped a huge bucket of water on you, for no damn reason. The sweat is salty and it burns your eyes as it constantly pours. The bed is all wet from the sweat and now you and your sweaty lover body is all sticky from their nasty ass sweat. The crazy part is they know they sweat to damn much they should have a towel handy to constantly wipe themselves as the sweat pour. But no they act like they don't have a sweating problem and they try to ignore it.

Have you experience a horrible sweaty episode before? Or did you not mind?

_____
_____
_____
_____

The Best and Worst 50 Sexual Experiences Ever

33. TOUCH AND BUST LOVER

Description: The Touch and Bust Lover is a Lover that has a major problem. The touch and bust lover cum too quickly during sex. Three pumps possibly the max five they already saying they are having an orgasm. Now let's be clear having an orgasm is great but not when you're ready to quit after five minutes. The key is to have multiple orgasms while being able to continue so you and your mate will be satisfied. Do not be selfish or a quitter. Eventually your lover will get fed up and cheat on you with someone who has a impeccable sex drive and who can stay in the race for the long haul or they will have a adult toy take your place. Regardless you are left alone. You will be alone with your sad, sad, sad Touch and Bust lonely self. Practice trying to last, if you can't do whatever you can to make sure your mate is satisfied also.

Have you ever had an experience with a touch and bust lover before? What were some things you did to spice up the relationship or to help them not have a orgasm so fast or to please yourself after they cum and they were ready to fall asleep and leave you up woke hot and bothered? How long did

The Best and Worst 50 Sexual Experiences Ever

the relationship last? Was the touch and bust lover the cause for the break up or for your current issues?

_____
_____
_____
_____

The Best and Worst 50 Sexual Experiences Ever

34. NOT YOUR OWN LOVER

Description: You and this person have amazing sex and heartfelt conversations and they are your ideal partner. Your family loves them they are a very accomplished person inside and out. You cannot imagine your life without this person. You want to live the rest of your life with them. You want to have kids with them and share your life with this special someone. But unfortunately you can't because they already have someone. They are already married to their life partner at least legally. They already have the house the kids and dog and white picket fence with someone else. Therefore they're not your own lover. Now in most cases people in a situation like this admire their ideal mate from a far or keep all the feelings they have for this person bottled up inside. But other people like myself, don't judge me. Have became very good friends with someone rather knowing or unknowing the other person's relationship status. Meaning you was aware that they are dating someone or married to someone at the time you and them became friends and you allowed nature to take its course for your own selfish personal reasons or after you fell in love with this person

The Best and Worst 50 Sexual Experiences Ever

you found out that they were not single and you continued to deal with them even though now you are a accessory to the infidelity. Keep in mind it takes two to be involved not just one. So in this type of situation either one of two things can happen. One you can end up actually being with this person meaning the other party will break up with their mate, the current wife, husband, boyfriend or girlfriend and have a relationship with you, but let's face it this rarely happens and if it does you will always wonder will they or are they possibly cheating on you or will they leave you for someone else also. Or number two you will spend most of your good years with this person hoping and wishing and praying on the possibility that they will leave their current spouse for you, being alone on holidays and crying those lonely nights because your dedicated your heart and life to someone that is not completely yours and eventually you wake up and you realize that you deserve better or they realize they cannot nor will not lose their current family because of dealing with you, regardless of your broken heart and you have lost a year, two or three being dedicated to the wrong person. The choice is yours.

The Best and Worst 50 Sexual Experiences Ever

Have you been in this type of situation before? Were you the one cheating or getting cheated on or were you the one in the middle of the whole situation? Were you part of the reason for the infidelity? How did the situation turn out for you based on your position in the relationship?

_____
_____
_____

The Best and Worst 50 Sexual Experiences Ever

35. BAD FELLATIO GIVER

Description: A male or female who performs the worst oral you have ever had. This person has no type of skills or any direction when it comes to giving oral stimulation. The bad fellatio giver have to be trained or taught to perform oral stimulation the proper way so that it can be the most affective. Practice makes perfect! So ladies grab you an erotic DVD, a banana, an ice cream cone even a lollipop will do and practice on the skill and techniques needed to please your man. Guys you can grab an erotic DVD as well and a peach or a strawberry or even a pear and get your techniques and skills together. When you feel like you are ready call that special someone and go for it. You must give it your all don't be lazy and don't be selfish with giving because when it's your turn to receive you want the person to give it all they got as well. It's a must that you enjoy giving oral sex to your mate because they can tell when

The Best and Worst 50 Sexual Experiences Ever

you don't like it and you are only doing it because they want you to. Get your skills together and make your partner have an orgasm like never before. Unfortunately, for you there is someone else out there like myself that loves to pleasure their mate on a daily basis orally and not just on holidays or special occasions.

Have you ever had this type of lover before? Did you teach them and help them learn how to pleasure you orally? Did you just break up with them?

_____
_____
_____
_____

The Best and Worst 50 Sexual Experiences Ever

36. The Bragging Lover

Description: The bragging lover is a person that claims they are the best at having sex. During your casual dates and conversations they constantly say how great they are in bed. They talk about how they can make you cum so many times and have you screaming for more. The man claim he has the biggest dick ever and the female may say her pussy gets wet like a water fountain. But when you finally get to the bedroom and have sex with the person the sex is nowhere close to how they said it would be. The sex was boring and bland. I would say false advertisement. Usually a person that has a great sex game does not have to announce it to you or the world. They just let the actions show in the bedroom. Most of the time great lovers will be humble, and totally catch you off guard in the bedroom. They will leave you wanting for more.

The Best and Worst 50 Sexual Experiences Ever

Have you had a situation with a lover that bragged and then it was the worst sex ever? How did you handle that situation? Did you voice your opinion or did you just keep your feelings to yourself?

_____
_____
_____
_____

The Best and Worst 50 Sexual Experiences Ever

37. GOSSIP LOVER

Description: The Gossip Lover is a lover that simply talks to damn much. As soon as you go on a date or you kiss this person or have sex with them they have to tell the whole universe that you and them had or have a intimate situation going on.

This person tells all of his or her family and friends. Co-workers or teammates they post pictures of you and them on social media such as Saturday date night putting a post up saying "with my boo". Even pictures of you sleeping that you haven't even seen nor agreed to. This person may even call and tell the media. No one likes a person who constantly run their mouth especially when both of you have not discussed the relationship or whatever the situation is. I think a discussion should be made before the world knows all of your business.

The Best and Worst 50 Sexual Experiences Ever

How did you address this situation and the person? Have you request or demand them to stop talking to the world about the contact you have made with them and also have you suggest or told them to take the pictures down off of social media or were you flattered?

_____
_____
_____
_____

The Best and Worst 50 Sexual Experiences Ever

38. EXTRA HAIRY LOVER

Description: An extra hairy male of female that just have to much damn body hair. A male may have an over hairy back, chest and shoulders or the woman may be overly natural with hair under her arms, legs and vaginal area. Some women may have a mustache or chin hair maybe even a full grown beard. Some people like this type of lover, which ever your personal preference is I'm all for it. But my preference is no hair. So I'm placing the extra hair lover on my worst list.

Do you rather have sex with a hairy lover or a shaved lover?

_____
_____
_____
_____

The Best and Worst 50 Sexual Experiences Ever

39. STIFF LOVER

Description: The stiff lover does not work in the bedroom. They do not contribute anything while the sexual activities are happening they are just laying there in one position and allowing you do all of the work. This lover don't throw it back, they don't give you any type of affection no hip movement nothing. They are just simply lazy and boring.

Have you had a stiff lover before? Did you stay in the relationship or did you cheat or just leave the stiff lover?

_____
_____
_____
_____

The Best and Worst 50 Sexual Experiences Ever

40. LATE CREEPER LOVER

Description: The late creeper lover is a lover that only calls you between the hours of 12:30 am and 4:30 am just to have sex with you sometimes they may stay over, and sometimes they will leave right after they have an orgasm. You only speak to this person when they want to have sex. They do not take you on any dates. This lover does not contact you or even check on you to see how you are doing. When you call them in the day or in the early part of the evening they do not answer your calls nor answer your texts.

Have you dealt with this type of lover before? Or the unattainable mate was exactly what you needed or wanted at the time? Why?

_____
_____
_____
_____

The Best and Worst 50 Sexual Experiences Ever

41. ONE SIDED LOVER

Description: The one sided lover is a lover that do not respect the saying "Do Unto Others As You Will Have Them Do Unto You." They want you to give them the best oral ever but when it's their turn they act as if they are tired or they just don't want to. Then when you tell them you are going on strike and you refuse to give them oral until they start doing it to you they have the nerve to get mad at you. When you have been doing your due diligence, and good deed all along pleasing them and making them happy inside and outside of the bedroom.

How long did you stay in this situation? Your partner acts of being one sided have they changed or have you left the situation?
_____
_____
_____

The Best and Worst 50 Sexual Experiences Ever

42. PROCRASTINATED LOVER

Description: Procrastinated lover is a lover is a lover that you are friends with first. You date them for 90 days and you really get to know them before you have sex with them just like your parents, society and Steve Harvey say do. Somehow along the way possibly between the fifteenth and twentieth date which possibly may be between the eightieth or ninety days you actually start to lose sexual interest and you just want to be friends. You no longer have that spark when you see that special someone. When they touch you or kiss you, you no longer want to rip their clothes off instantly. You stop fantasizing about having your first sexual encounter with them because you procrastinated and now you have entered the friend zone.

The Best and Worst 50 Sexual Experiences Ever

Have this situation ever happen to you? Did you or would you just have sex with them on the fifth date or hell possibly even the first night? Or are you happy with the results from the ninety day rule?

_____
_____
_____
_____

The Best and Worst 50 Sexual Experiences Ever

43. ALIEN LOVER

Description: Alien lover is a lover that totally turns into a different person during sex or after they may have an orgasm. As soon as you start making love to them or when they are having a orgasm their eyes may start to roll or they legs may begin to shake they may begin to yell out crazy things you have never even heard of. Words that may make no sense at all, the alien lover may put so many marks, bites and scratches on you while having sex or a orgasm. The alien lover may even jump out of bed onto the floor while having an orgasm or may even say the famous words of "don't touch me".

What are some out of the normal things you or your alien lover have done during sex or while have an orgasm?

_____
_____
_____

The Best and Worst 50 Sexual Experiences Ever

44. TINY PENIS LOVER

Description: A tiny penis lover is a lover with a very small penis. This lover penis is so small that you barely know that it is there nor can you feel it in your vagina or while you are having anal sex with them. During sex the small penis will not stay in because it's so small while he is on top or while having sex doggy style. Unfortunately this situation is beyond the man's control, he was born this way but there are some things you can purchase to help out with this unfortunate situation. You can purchase a penis pump, a penis extension from your local store also possibly forms of vitamins or pills that may possibly help the man extend the size of his penis. Of course the male should check with his doctor to make sure the pills are healthy for him to take.

The Best and Worst 50 Sexual Experiences Ever

Have you experienced a situation with this type of lover before? What are some things you and your lover did to make the situation better?

_____
_____
_____
_____

The Best and Worst 50 Sexual Experiences Ever

45. BOOTY CALL LOVER

Description: A booty call lover is a lover that only contacts you to have sex. This lover does not stay over after sex. You will not go on any dates with this lover because they don't respect nor think of you in that manner. The booty call lover will never meet any of your family nor your friends because they only want to have sex with you and nothing more.

Have you had a relationship with booty call lover before? How long you dealt with this person? Did you have any idea that you were just their booty call?

_____
_____
_____
_____

The Best and Worst 50 Sexual Experiences Ever

46. BAD KISSER

Description: A bad kisser is someone who simply does not know how to kiss in the correct manner. The bad kisser lips and tongue are not in the correct place it needs to be while being kissed.

How did you cope and manage to make a situation better with a bad kisser?

_____
_____
_____
_____

The Best and Worst 50 Sexual Experiences Ever

47. ARCHIVED PENIS LOVER

Description: Archived penis lover is a lover or lovers that you have been having a sexual relationship or a long amount of time usually years. This lover is a lover that always stays in the shadows no matter how many relationships you may have that may come and go. This lover will always be there for you when you need them as a friend and sexually. This lover is basically placed on the shelf and taken down or break glass in case of emergency when needed. This lover know how make you cum like no other and they know where all your hot spots are. You feel comfortable with this lover. You may have even lost relationships with other people over this lover.

The Best and Worst 50 Sexual Experiences Ever

Have you ever let an archived lover come between relationships with someone else you were trying to get to know? How long have you been dealing with your archived lover?

_____
_____
_____
_____

The Best and Worst 50 Sexual Experiences Ever

48. UNCLEAN LOVER

Description: A lover that does not take their hygiene as seriously as they should. You and your lover may be in a hot and ready to have sex and the partner may go down to give the male fellatio and his ball and penis is musty or salty or a female vagina has a unclean smell that should be fixed immediately that goes for the male and female anus as well. All portions of the private area should be kept up to standards especially if you will like to receive oral pleasure.

Have you had an experience with a unclean lover before? How did you handle that uncomfortable situation?

_____
_____
_____
_____

The Best and Worst 50 Sexual Experiences Ever

49. PARANOID LOVER

Description: A paranoid lover is a lover that is scared to do anything new during sex. This lover do not want to try any new positions, this lover do not want to have nor try to have oral sex. The paranoid lover act as if they are allergic to sperm when the male partner say they want to cum in the mouth or on the paranoid lover face or when a female offers to cum in a paranoid lover mouth when they are about to have a orgasm. This lover never wants to do anything spontaneous sexually and they are scared to have sex in public because they are afraid they will be seen by others. Are they are afraid to be tied up or handcuffed in the bed room because they think its bad luck? All these qualities are symptoms of a paranoid lover.

Have you had a relationship with a paranoid lover? How long did you stay in the relationship? Did the paranoid lover change

The Best and Worst 50 Sexual Experiences Ever

their ways or did it take a toll on the relationship?

_____
_____
_____
_____

The Best and Worst 50 Sexual Experiences Ever

50. THE ROUGH SEX LOVER

Description: The rough sex lover is someone that loves to have rough sex. While making love with the rough sex lover this person may be too deep in the vagina or thrusting you too hard to the point you're sore after having sex with them. The rough sex lover may spank you to hard or pull your hair too hard during sex. They may scratch bite too much to the point having sex with the rough lover is no longer fun. You start to focus on the pain more than the pleasure while having sex with the rough lover.

What are some things your rough lover did to you while having sex? Have you ever been a rough lover? If so what are some things you did to improve the relationship so it would be pleasurable for you and your partner?

_____
_____
_____

The Best and Worst 50 Sexual Experiences Ever

What are some of your worst sexual experiences off the list I created? Do you have any of your own?

_____
_____
_____
_____
_____
_____
_____
_____

The Best and Worst 50 Sexual Experiences Ever

Chapter 3
SEXUAL EXPERIENCES SEX JOURNAL

_____
_____
_____
_____
_____
_____
_____

The Best and Worst 50 Sexual Experiences Ever

SEXUAL EXPERIENCES SEX JOURNAL

_____
_____
_____
_____
_____
_____
_____
_____

The Best and Worst 50 Sexual Experiences Ever

SEXUAL EXPERIENCES SEX JOURNAL

_____
_____
_____
_____
_____
_____
_____

The Best and Worst 50 Sexual Experiences Ever

SEXUAL EXPERIENCES SEX JOURNAL

_____
_____
_____
_____
_____
_____
_____
_____

The Best and Worst 50 Sexual Experiences Ever

SEXUAL EXPERIENCES SEX JOURNAL

_____
_____
_____
_____
_____
_____
_____

The Best and Worst 50 Sexual Experiences Ever

SEXUAL EXPERIENCES SEX JOURNAL

_____
_____
_____
_____
_____
_____
_____

The Best and Worst 50 Sexual Experiences Ever

SEXUAL EXPERIENCES SEX JOURNAL

_____
_____
_____
_____
_____
_____
_____

The Best and Worst 50 Sexual Experiences Ever

SEXUAL EXPERIENCES SEX JOURNAL

_____
_____
_____
_____
_____
_____
_____

The Best and Worst 50 Sexual Experiences Ever

SEXUAL EXPERIENCES SEX JOURNAL

_____
_____
_____
_____
_____
_____
_____

The Best and Worst 50 Sexual Experiences Ever

SEXUAL EXPERIENCES SEX JOURNAL

_____
_____
_____
_____
_____
_____
_____

The Best and Worst 50 Sexual Experiences Ever

SEXUAL EXPERIENCES SEX JOURNAL

_____
_____
_____
_____
_____
_____
_____
_____

The Best and Worst 50 Sexual Experiences Ever

SEXUAL EXPERIENCES SEX JOURNAL

_____
_____
_____
_____
_____
_____
_____

The Best and Worst 50 Sexual Experiences Ever

SEXUAL EXPERIENCES SEX JOURNAL

_____
_____
_____
_____
_____
_____
_____
_____

The Best and Worst 50 Sexual Experiences Ever

SEXUAL EXPERIENCES SEX JOURNAL

_____
_____
_____
_____
_____
_____
_____

The Best and Worst 50 Sexual Experiences Ever

CHAPTER 4
MY MONTHLY SEX GOALS TO IMPROVE MY SEX LIFE.

The Best and Worst 50 Sexual Experiences Ever

JANUARY:

_____
_____
_____
_____
_____
_____
_____

The Best and Worst 50 Sexual Experiences Ever

FEBRUARY:

_____
_____
_____
_____
_____
_____
_____

The Best and Worst 50 Sexual Experiences Ever

MARCH:

_____
_____
_____
_____
_____
_____
_____

The Best and Worst 50 Sexual Experiences Ever

APRIL:

_____
_____
_____
_____
_____
_____
_____

The Best and Worst 50 Sexual Experiences Ever

MAY:

_____
_____
_____
_____
_____
_____
_____
_____

The Best and Worst 50 Sexual Experiences Ever

JUNE:

_____
_____
_____
_____
_____
_____
_____
_____

The Best and Worst 50 Sexual Experiences Ever

JULY:

_____
_____
_____
_____
_____
_____
_____

The Best and Worst 50 Sexual Experiences Ever

AUGUST:

_____
_____
_____
_____
_____
_____
_____

The Best and Worst 50 Sexual Experiences Ever

SEPTEMBER:

_____
_____
_____
_____
_____
_____
_____

The Best and Worst 50 Sexual Experiences Ever

OCTOBER:

_____
_____
_____
_____
_____
_____
_____

The Best and Worst 50 Sexual Experiences Ever

NOVEMBER:

_____
_____
_____
_____
_____
_____
_____

The Best and Worst 50 Sexual Experiences Ever

DECEMBER:

_____
_____
_____
_____
_____
_____
_____

The Best and Worst 50 Sexual Experiences Ever

Hello Reader,

Thank you to everyone who has purchased my book! I wanted to create a book that everyone could relate to no matter what your sexual preference choice is. I love sex especially great sex.
I hope this book makes a great conversation piece at parties, dates and as gifts.

Sincerely,
K. Marie

The Best and Worst 50 Sexual Experiences Ever

www.ingramcontent.com/pod-product-compliance
Lightning Source LLC
LaVergne TN
LVHW021407080426
835508LV00020B/2479